ETERNITY ON HOLD

.

MARIO SUSKO

■

ETERNITY ON HOLD

■

TURTLE POINT PRESS

■

NEW YORK

■

2005

■

COPYRIGHT © 2005 BY TURTLE POINT PRESS

LCCN 2004107985   ISBN 1-885586-34-5

DESIGN AND COMPOSITION BY
WILSTED & TAYLOR PUBLISHING SERVICES

PRINTED IN CANADA

CONTENTS

PART ONE (OF TWO)

.

die Angst, dass ich mich verraten könnte

und alles das sagen, wovor ich mich

fürchte, und die Angst, dass ich nichts

sagen könnte, weil alles unsagbar ist—

RAINER MARIA RILKE

LIFE

Grandmother and I shared a small crammed room.
I slept on the sofa, she, in a high white bed.
She died when I was thirteen years old.
It was a cold gray January afternoon,
the kind that made your nostrils glue together
and the eyes burn from the coal smoke
belched by asthmatic chimneys in the street.

I came back from school and found my aunt
sitting on a rickety chair in the hall.
She pressed my stiff hands against her cheeks,
whispering, You'll be alone tonight, my dear,
but I thought only of her soft velvet skin.

She took me into the room and to the bed
where my grandmother lay in her long blue dress,
with a small bouquet of satin violets on the pillow
and two wavering candles on the marble top table.
The curtains were drawn, the wall mirror covered.

It was grandma's shoes that kept me transfixed,
pointed black caps sticking up like crows' beaks,
and when my aunt went to close the cupboard door
which always squeaked open mysteriously on its own
I spat silently three times to chase away bad luck.

The cupboard was a giant magic hat, things inside,
never seen, like a gold rabbit's foot she smuggled
through the German checkpoint, an endless source
of her night stories. After each she'd kiss me
and say softly, Adesso dormi e fai un bel sogno.

My mother was to arrive by a late train, so I
had to sleep at my place. I stood guard, the major
in the third room, requisitioned for war veterans
by the commissariat, listening to patriotic airs.
I pretended to be asleep when mother tiptoed in.

I tried to remember every song my grandmother sang
to me in Italian, about her homeland, lost love,
and that morning I awoke in the frigid room, alone,
with a shameful erection. I propped myself up,
looking at her waxed face, and saw her wink at me.

Two days later I raided the cupboard, digging
out a pistol lighter, cancelled banknotes, letters,
sepia photos of sailing ships, a cracked telescope,
an old broken compass; I got so angry I ran down
to the shed in the yard, dragged out my treasure,
a wobbly corroding bike with no brakes, and rode it
around the oak tree until I was blinded by tears.

THE SMELL

I'd hide my soul between the starched sheets
in the cupboard, safe to be among rose
petals, dry lavender stalks, and mothballs,
when mother sent me out to look for him,
and I ran along the barbed wire, my body
enmeshed in the shadows of haulage cables,
my eyes burning in the glow of the steelworks.

I never found him, but in every barroom I
sneaked into I smelled his sweat, heard
his laughter, recognized his hairy hand
around a woman's neck, pulling her head
back, not like my mother's, while she,
feigning reluctance, shrieked jocundly.
I'd push my way out, convinced he saw me,

and take a shortcut home, zigzagging
among boxcars at the ghostly switch yard
like a hunted rabbit, across garden plots,
while dogs' barking echoed in my ears,
and his panting infested my slimy nostrils.
She'd sit in the kitchen, knitting, look
at me with her ravished eyes, and say,

You failed again. Go wash off that smell.
I waited motionless in a frost-covered bed

for my soul to come to me and end the shivers,
staring at the lustful flames breathe
in the window pane, until a shell flash
blinded me, blowing away the cupboard, and
I scrambled up from the dank cement floor
in the basement, an aged man, trailing
the odor of blood and scorched flesh.

THE TUNNEL

a skinny kid following his mother,
    dragging a small burlap sack,
    intent on finding shiny cartridges,
    insignia, gas masks, anything
    his imagination willed to be there,
as she collected pieces of coal
walking the railroad tracks,
her head swaying left and right,
the rhythm of some forlorn bird.

precious black stones fallen off
a tender to make the water boil
with potatoes that tossed and turned
like his first ball, lost but going
nowhere in the river's mad trough,

the best to be found in the tunnel
that loomed ahead, the gaping mouth
of a whale, though she never dared
enter it again, and he remembered
the coughs, the sweat, the whispers
when townspeople had been herded in,
then strung against the wall to wait
for the armored train to screech along,
two crimson eyes that burned forever

through the smoke making him
choke and let the warm fluid
course down his shivering legs.

then the new line was built
on the other side of the town,
the old tracks and ties removed,
the dirt soon trampled by peasants
taking a shortcut with their carts,
baskets, bundles to the market place.

he would come after the school,
before the procession of ghosts
traveled back, listen to the flutter
of bats, soft sobbing sounds, the bark:
ruhe, the cocking, and finally the rumble
storm through his brain, drowning out
everything else, yet at the end
he'd emerge victoriously, without a drop
having trickled down his legs.

INHERITANCE

My grandfather died
sitting on a stone bench. Sent down
to fetch him, I walked around and stood
in front of him, but he still gazed
at the sea, his mouth half open
as if he wanted to tell me something.

I sat quietly next to him,
hoping I could locate the same spot,
the same wave traveling toward us,
slowly and patiently, like an animal
coming to get us both
and carry off to that other land beyond.

I saw him again escape from the transport
train into a lake and hide among the reeds;
he sucked the air through a straw
while the guard dogs barked at the moon
double and he clutched his heart
that flapped against the yellow star.

His left fist was clenched, but I noticed
a little yellowish triangle sticking out,
the beak of some small bird that hid there,

waiting for my grandfather to set it free.
He could never open his hands fully,
his knuckles having become tree knots.

So, I sat there and he sort of leaned
against me, two passengers on a ship
that rocked gently toward the setting sun.
Then suddenly I jumped up, snatched the bird
from his fist, and started to run up the path.
When I glanced back, the bench was empty,
except for two battered boots underneath
that one day, I knew, would belong to me.

THE ALL

as a child I thought eternity
began whenever I stopped to count
the invisible stars in my room
because I ran out of numbers
trying to outpace the squeaking
of iron springs behind the paper wall.

when I kissed my grandmother's cheek,
her skin smelling of churned butter,
I knew she wasn't dead for I too
could lie in my bed with a wooden cross
in my hands and hold my breath forever.

I believed pregnant women were smugglers,
carrying, after the war, sacks of potatoes
or coal under their dress, and I learned
through fear, having seen a horse drop
out of a horse, I hadn't come from an egg.

there was so much unlearning
later on to be done, about the suitcase
full of maps with shortcuts to life

after life, a tree that could hide
its shadow, and words bring salvation
when ripeness starved its fruits to death.

sleeping in a different bed every night
to outguess random targets practitioners,
I came to see the all as a counted nothing.

THE EGG

Say three Our Fathers to have
A soft-boiled egg done right,
mother would say, and I said four,
even five, slowly, when I thought
I had sinned looking at the photos
of naked women father kept
in his fishing bag, for I believed
that would strengthen my faith.
Mother's eggs always came out rawish,
with the whites resembling mucus
that would ooze out of the nose
of a kid across the street, whom I
loved to cheat at the game of marbles.
Anyway, mother's eggs, I construed
impartially, were like that because she,
in fact, prayed to Mary instead.

One morning while she was staring
at the egg that bounced in the water,
and her lips were moving silently,
I ventured my long prepared remark:
The teacher said God would never be
Able to tell us whether he created
A chicken or an egg first. Do you know?
She slapped me and said: Don't you

Ever ask me those stupid dialectical
Marxist questions again. This school
Poisons your head. God help us all.

But I wanted to know what negated
what, so I decided to be a Marxist.
I refused to eat eggs, chicken,
or any kind of meat because that meant
oppressing other living creatures.
While recuperating from para-typhus,
I kept my mouth tightly shut,
making my mother cry as she held
the plate with chicken soup in her lap.

In school I surpassed even my teacher
declaiming about the exploitation
of the masses, the corruption of the rich
who could afford caviar and frog's legs
and the proletariat only cabbage and beans.
One day the teacher called me
to his desk: Where is all this fervor
Coming from, he whispered. It's the egg
And the chicken, sir. He pointed stiffly
to the corner and I stood there sweating
and inhaling the damp flaky paint.

After the class, when everyone else
was gone, he said gently: Come here.
Enough of that dialectical crap
Of yours, you hear me? What you get
In school is for the world; what you

Believe in is for you. Listen well,
God in his infinite wisdom created
The egg and the chicken simultaneously.
How's that for an explanation?

And he motioned with his crooked finger
to the door. Instantly my whole world
crumbled down. I ran home and asked
that night for scrambled eggs. Mother
crossed herself, mumbling sorrowfully:
Lord, please help me with this boy.

The following morning I opened
the cupboard and took out two eggs;
I let them boil till the water
evaporated and I went hoarse praying.

FEEDING

mother never stopped cooking
for my father,
as if one day he would show up,
sit at the table
and ask me, How was school today?

I had to eat for two,
the measure of her purpose in life
not to be destroyed,
though I knew that after every meal
her forlorn look would make me vomit.

then, on my eighteenth birthday, she
stopped. from that day on, come dinner
time, she'd say, Food is in the freezer.
she'd take her bag of cookies and a box
of chocolates and disappear in her room.

with my first honorarium in hand
I went to the city's fanciest restaurant,
ordered two full courses and gorged myself,
belching in turns, once for me, once
for my mother, all the way home.

METAPHORPLICATION

twenty men that cross
a bridge declaring themselves
are twenty men advancing
if there's a bridge to cross

otherwise there are twenty
bridges in twenty minds respectively
and the river's presence
is of no real consequence

do they cross barefoot
do they cross in boots
will they break villagers' bread
will they break villagers' head

a man on the other bank
sees twenty men cross a bridge
then blows up twenty bridges
just to be on the safe side

he goes back to his village
which is now twenty villages
and he is twenty men with twenty dogs
and wives and gods respectively

DYEING

it's Friday / a black car
oozes down the street / inside
a man in a black leather
overcoat / a crow hops onto
the sidewalk eyeing a black
glass button that glints
among small pieces of coal /
the windows are painted
black with streaks resembling
cicatrices / a woman's head
in a black hat pops out
through a door frame and
quickly withdraws / a black
glove on the drain cover
dances with a curb hugging
runnel / one black shoe hangs
on the cast iron fence /
the car rolls slowly to
a stop at the soot blackened
railroad parapet I cannot jump
over
        / I stand pinned there
like a butterfly / the radiator
breathing warm air into

my face / I am to die
in the next frame /
                    but
a voice behind the spotlights
yells, "Cut. Let's wrap it up
for today."
                / it's Sunday
and I am on my way home; the man
in the black leather overcoat
stands in front of my house;
two blurry faces in a jeep
sit like clay figures; there
are no cameras, no fill-in
lights, no cables; I do not see
a clapper boy; the street is
empty and I do not carry
the capsule which I had under
my white shirt to stain it
red after the blast; my wife
on the fourth floor balcony
flails her hands Go! Go!
but I see no need to turn
around and run;
                    I approach
him, trying to figure out why
he is there, in that black leather
overcoat, yet without make-up;
"We decided to change the location
and dye things more realistically,"
he says and laughs; I stare at

the gun in his hand, the barrel
pointing down, his finger tapping
rhythmically the trigger guard;
it is real, yet, for some reason,
the only thing I can think about
is the effect blood is going to have
now that I wear my red shirt /

CONVERSION

I came upon a man in black who sat on a tank,
tending his sheep that grazed impassively
around the craters and among dead bodies.

I am looking for my son, I said squinting.
The bullets in his cartridge belt slung
over his shoulder shone in the sun like teeth.

He smiled, chewing a cigarette to the other
corner of his mouth, and motioned with his hand
to the field. Plenty to choose from, he said.

The sheep were moving away toward the shade
of a big oak tree, the bodies following
on all fours. I strained my ears to hear the bell

I knew. He slid down and stared at me.
Is that your stomach growling, he asked.
I am just trying to find my son, I whispered.

You want me to shoot one? He spat out the butt
and stomped it with his boot that was like my son's.
We are talking about some good meat, he grinned.

The shirt looked familiar, but I couldn't tell.
My sheep started to fan out and I suddenly heard
a dog yelp behind me. He whistled, the sound

thin and piercing, making the bodies stop.
I felt the sweat run down my buttocks and legs,
as if someone was punching holes in my ribs.

Have you seen my son, I uttered, not knowing
whether any sound left my mouth. You never had
a son, he yelled and cocked his submachine gun.

The boots were the same, and so was the shirt.
And the Mickey Mouse watch on his wrist was the same.
Tell you what, he said and laughed. I'll be your son.

BEYOND

Eternity is God's oblivion, you said,
a faint smile crossing your lips.
That's why we are left with history,
not to forget what we cannot be.

you were taping your grandmother's bracelet,
a gold arabesque snake, onto your abdomen,
and I could see four or five hairs
curling upward, as if trying to explore
the air above the waistband of your panties,
two silver rings you'd already parted with
lying like eyeballs on the bare kitchen table.

Futile words and useless acts, I thought,
we needed to assuage the fear. Not
of dying but living the absence of living,
like a frog I once saw on television
that suspends its being through the winter.

the following morning you left the city,
your face behind a fogged bus window
a featureless apparition, forcing me
to feel my chapped lips and blow you a kiss.

two days later I managed to climb
into the attic of an abandoned building
and peer stupidly through my binoculars
at the checkpoint, praying that I see
your rings on the guard's fingers,
for that would have meant you were safe,
somewhere beyond our crazed reasoning.

a figure that leaned in perfect harmony
with his ak-47 against a barrel
smoked a cigarette, his derisive stare
telling me he somehow sensed I was there,
then stretched his arms, and I saw only
two blackleathered fists up in the air.

FEAR

I was crouching in the cellar
leaning against the wall
that thudded like my heart,
trying to read a book,
and when I started to turn
the page it became
a thin concrete slab.
I managed to lift it a bit
and there was a pit underneath,
my father there, his eyes
a vitrified stare, nostrils
like two slits, lips puckered
resembling a sturgeon's,
his left arm around the neck
of a young naked woman
who looked at me and said,
Don't you recognize me?
I'm your mother, she laughed.
And so is every woman here
To the left and right of us.
She stretched her arm,
the fingers clawing at my flesh,
and pulled me flirtingly in.
You'll be safe down here.
And then the blast buried us.

I came around, ants still
stinging my eyelids, blood
from my nose guiding me
to the door and into the yard
filled with children
whose wasted shadows chased
crimson balloons whirling
in the wind and the veils of dust.
I stumbled over a body and fell.
This is a bad dream, I thought,
or heard the figure whisper.
A hand grabbed my ankle.
Save yourself while you can.
And I began to crawl blindly,
dragging my mother's voice
across the blistering blacktop.

I am afraid to sleep now,
for I may wake up again
to find out I have gone west.

THE UN-WOR‿LDS

it is, perhaps,
too late now to learn
about life with the un-
verbs
un:chain my heart
un:button your blouse
un:dress me naked
un:leash your passion
un:bosom your feelings
un:shell your thoughts
un:wind yourself
un:fetter my soul

I lived,
perhaps too long,
with the verbs of the un-
world:
unbar every door
unhouse every living thing
unbuild every house
unpeople the valley
unarm the children if necessary
unnerve them to the point of madness
undo every evidence
unbind the dead only

What there is we think is
ours in those prefixes
and suffixes:
the will to create
through a reversal,
the power to reverse
through obliteration

—the signs always given
always misread willfully
in the corrupted history
of our geography,
in the cursed geography
of our history

: when seeking to mend
is overthrowing and ravishing
then? O, Lord,
unhouse my mind
undo my memory
to undie me

COLLATERAL

if i have run out
of words / the measure of my own
being / and there is nothing
left to go by / by memory
/ which is what for which what
is not : in the elliptical silence
of pain / i will not move / and
thus i will escape / my mother's fate /

the radial artery giving up /
blood / slowly / eaten by itself
life becoming charted percentages /
to be glanced at / in passing
/ a tightrope walking : the eyes
converging / at a zero balance
which is what for which what
is / a benumbing light / fixed /

switched off though still punctuated
/ on the retina's wall : a dot /
mirrored / measured / then voided /

i have blinked and thus moved / not
realizing i'd have to tell a story
without words : stare
at my own image / in the mirror /
signifying collateral damage

BALANCE

maybe some twenty years from now
they'll sit down with their adversaries
and over coffee and assorted drinks
exchange notes and peruse the maps,
entertaining bald historians and strategists
with their now polite explanations
why they had to kill each other.

the atmosphere at a peaceful resort
will be cordial, even some jokes offered
to unburden the collective conscience
while discussing the variables of life
and death that once had to create
the shortest distance between them.

places such as Pig's Head, Turtle Point,
Goat's Trail will be revisited, coordinates
re-examined, hands that held the wheel
or hovered above the button will try to be
steady again as the memory searches
for the orgasmic explosion of color particles.

I have now dead future pictures
to show, any unmarked grave that could
be my mother's, any lit window once mine,

as I sit in a dark empty room in a town
pinpointed on some waterproof map
and hold the eviction notice in my hand,
the droning of the landlord's refrigerator
reminding my displaced mind of gravity.

commentators will then talk about the need
to understand the necessary historical balance
in the global scheme of things, and mention
in passing only the unbalanced act of someone
who throws a good refrigerator out of the window
and jumps, trying to beat it to the ground.

ROTATION

The room is dark and empty,
but there is no more a smell
of death peeling off the concrete
(though he couldn't really say
what that smell would now be,
of rank clothes and the sweat,
gun powder mixed with the burn,
the morning breath and the urine
in the farthest corner of the cellar)

He takes off his shoes and lies down
on his belly, staring at the slit
the hall light makes between the floor
and the door frame, convinced
two black bulbs are someone's toe-caps
(though he cannot quite accept
that anyone would be standing there
again, waiting for him to lose
his composure and yell, Who's there?)

He gets up, his breath choking him,
and looks wide-eyed through the peephole;
there's no figure, no face, only
the hall disappearing in a dim blur
(though he doesn't want to contemplate

why someone would be crouching indiscreetly,
whether the shoes size could be that
of a midget, or whether this time
they've sent such a person to get him)

He ties the laces and slings his shoes
around the neck, wraps himself
in a blanket and lies down again, his mind
forcing his eyes to make the caps fade away
(though he knows that when he wakes up
in the morning and yanks the door open,
there will be no one there, but someone
will walk in and push him out to wait
till the next day and try to get back in)

REARRANGEMENT

that last day I recalled:
hearing a bird suddenly go mute
in the middle of its song,
seeing a squirrel freeze half-way
across the sagging power line:

the briefest of moments it was:
an eternity: when we wonder
what it is we want to remember
or forget, whether we are running
from death or to death: once again:

I myself caught in the bombed room,
trying to figure out whether one heard
the blast first and then realized
he had been shot, or the other way
round: as if that mattered after all:

for we had to talk ourselves
into believing: we had chosen right
when we had no choice: to survive
in the story whose beginning and end
was to be rearranged by each teller:

RAGE

everything in me is dead
except my mute rage.
the eyes, once daring acrobats,
are now clowns that make
the audience laugh each time
they squirt out distilled tears.
I have my umbrella to protect me
from exploding confetti shells
that rain down in all colors.

I do not talk. I have talked
too much to survive, said little.
the corners of my white mouth
loop down, the make-up extends
them upward in a frozen smile.
I run in circles pursued
by two playful beams of light,
and then the whistle makes me
fall, announcing the lion act.

my death is always entertaining,
for the silver threads strummed
by an occasional moth disappear,

and I am gone, forced one more time
not to recognize my torturers
who sit in civilian clothes now,
clean shaven, mindless of their past,
and hold their kids' popcorn
or juice ceremonially in their hands.

ESCAPE

it's a curse to remember
more than you can forget.

the sunbleached smudge
on the wall, your backward mirror   here/or/as/there

a shaft of light that collapses
into a blind dot, the last word   now/or/as/then

deoxygenated in the brain
making the nerves burn   as/if/if/is

under the skin, and the bubbles
on your lips burst like rose buds.   as/is/is/as

the only escape left becomes
dead sleep of the insomniac mind.

CASUALTY

it doesn't hurt anymore,
the life cut off above the knee
(Who the hell has got it now?)

a hollow voice from the loudspeaker
asks, Has he stepped on it?
someone in the corner whispers,
The nerves must be all damaged;
It won't do to stitch it back on.

the window lets in swishing twigs
and the mist, the light blares cold
(How old am I? When was I born?)

there is a child, one-legged puppet
pressed tightly to his skinny chest.
Mama, I do not want to go back.
a man in the doorway holds the knife.
I will show you what life is like.

a shell fells a tree in the yard,
two eggs in the nest fly to the sky
(I will not talk, I will not cry.)

No one can do anything about it,
he says, looking at the puppet
thrown in the bush. Life, I mean.
Can't just take it and hop away.
he wonders if it's a booby trap.

rubber gloves are red, like father's
holding sow's intestines in the sun
(Whereof the feeling if the nerves sleep?)

her long legs are spread in a dream
and she bends her knees, the sheet
becoming a tent, big enough for him
to lift one end and crawl in, inhaling
the moist almondy smell of escape.

a train whistle shoots through the air,
a chain saw rakes like a submachine gun
(I haven't walked far enough to forget.)

SUITCASES

in the act of throwing things
into a suitcase, those very things
you think will save you, or
some semblance of purpose,
that I used to see, as a child,
strewn along the roadsides:
a cap, a scarf, a snapshot,
sheets of paper with smeared ink,
a shoe—my question never answered:
why it always had to be just one—
an alarm clock, found once
smashed against a rock, handless,
similar to the one my grandfather
had put in his, strapped with a belt
from the previous war—and I
wondered whether that was sheer lunacy
or pure defiance, for he must
have known what the word relocation
meant—things that in the end
we may even hate because they make us
remember too much or too little

and when he came back, carrying
an empty wooden suitcase, he stripped
himself naked in the yard, put

inside his lice-infested clothes
and burned the whole thing, shivering
behind the wavering curtain of smoke

every year he would go out and buy
a suitcase: and when he died, he had
three under his bed, two on the chest,
four in the closet, one in the bathroom,
eight in the attic—Each of them, he
told me once, is full of memories,
for that only stands up to madness,
that and full, unadulterated readiness:

so I dragged my suitcase all the way
to these shores, the first one I managed
to grab, tied up with a rope, but I
could no longer say whether things
inside were mine or those I'd inherited,
thus having run from this or some other war—

and when I opened it, there were only
charred pieces there of what I took to be
my grandfather's clothes, and I realized
it was my memory that now wanted to forget
me, for I became a threat to its sanity—

A LEAP

what they wanted was tools
to assemble their collective memory,
instruments to readjust the maps,
and arrange their future oblivions.

you tried to offer them words, those
that revealed man's propensity
for manipulating truth and history
and thus escaped the text's corruption.

I sat in a windowless room, the answers
I'd memorized to inevitable questions
about one's guilt by association darting
in my mind like birds before the storm.

the first time I saw you you sat naked
on a rock jutting out of the lead-green
river and read a book, motionless
in the distance as if cut out in stone.

we expected better from you, they
said, a wet towel smelling of urine
sealing my eyes, and I floated downstream,
the back of my head scorched by the sun.

whatever I could have renounced then,
and whatever I could have imagined,
later on, whether you died before me, or
I before you was erased from the story.

in another life I found myself
standing on a bridge, the riverbed
a caked spiderwebbed mud, the bodies
heaped at the banks giant mating frogs.

to be at peace with the rock and see it
as truth, and the river as history
when neither could be there was a leap
into the light. I opened the book,
releasing the words and watching them
fly off, then removed my clothes and jumped.

THE PIT

cables above sticking out of the walls,
twisted snakes, headless and incrusted,

a small puddle at the bottom
of the pit, cold and sticky, flies

circling before my eyes, one landing
on my half-open mouth, exploring the taste,

my whole life arrested down there
staring at the cloudless shivering sky,

fingers digging into the dirt and mortar
that come off like warm pieces of flesh,

I try to figure out whether my mouth
or a pipe at my ear makes a whizzing sound,

whether I jumped in or was thrown in,
but the mind keeps buzzing: you are safe,

as long as you are down here, and come
stars you'll have no need of matches,

silver plumes concurring, curling upward,
their gelatine tentacles enticing me to follow,

I hear voices in the sky, streaming down,
gentle summer breeze that will cool my face,

and my dead mother's voice: I want you
to come up, you hear me, right now.

THE BLAST

a child running blindly
through endless doors in the mirror,
trying to flee the sound,

though it is the blast's echo,
already in the room, a tumor
fed by the ignorant blood,

its beating independent of the heart's,
that makes his head fly
into the glass and the skin crack

The lines drawn by invisible scalpels,
snake-like rays lashing out
from the hollow center that wells

red droplets It returns
an old man's face, its memory drowned
in his ear-drums' bursting deep

The son that had never existed
but always was, the woman
that was but had never been

The life turned weighted air
that imploded the moment the pitch
had been conceived and the body

swallowed its screaming dust
Scooped out it left a silent hole
with vessels neatly tied up,

the child, long forgotten in the reflection,
now deaf and mute, with howling eyes,
locked in the marbled stillness His image

DEATH

1.

the end is not where we want it
to be, the eyes playing tricks on us,
moving the horizon endlessly away

it is not what we imagine it
to be, the mind unable to lift
the weight of memory off the ground

1 A.

one day as a kid I asked my grandmother,
Are you dying, grandma? the fingers
of her right hand sticking toward me
like a claw ready to snatch my breath.

I've been dying all my life, she drawled,
her mouth becoming a crooked smile
that made me wince. What d'you think?
You're a big boy. Is it time I stop?

he was trying to tell me something,
each soundless word a bubble
bursting into weightless red dots.
I clasped his ears with my hands,

saying, It's all right.... and he arched
his back and let his breath go slowly
as if to make sure I'd inhale his life
still there and keep it safe in my mouth.

PART TWO (OF ONE)

.

Soy lo que sobrevive a los cobardes
Y a los fatuos que ha sido.

JORGE LUIS BORGES

DELIVERANCE

my talking was to deliver me from fear,
my gestures, from despair of being
forsaken, the messages like those of a dog
barking and wagging its tail, something
God by design makes us choose at random.

ill-prepared for the merchants of fate
I bought shadows at the market to throw off
my pursuers, but they followed my scent
to the river, flashlights ice-skating
on the surface, frogs in the reeds their music.

once across I watched my clothes float
downstream, hugging the rocks, uncoupling,
disappearing as if devoured by the river's
whirling maw. I scrubbed my skin
with mud and stones to have my memory

bleed away with the smell, as my eyes played
hide-and-seek with glow worms and tracers,
carrying me home to my bed to retrieve
a brick heated in the oven and wrapped
in my mother's old shawl to warm up my feet.

it was the gleaming steel sun in the morning
with two holes staring at my eyes when I
forced them open, and a voice of the shadow
that made the light disperse off its edges,
Shall I kill him or make him swim back,

and another, its fist sprinkling my forehead
with sand as if it passed from the bulb
of an hourglass, Let's hear his story first.
so I talked and wagged my tail through the woods
and the valleys, across the fields and the ocean.

THE STORY

an exile has only one story
to tell, over and over again,
which in the end begins, by the force
of repetition, to retell itself.

his mind then becomes nothing
but juggling hoops tossed up
in the air by invisible hands,
waiting for tigers to jump through.

it confuses timing and dimensions:
finds itself at the wrong place
at the right time, or vice versa,
it measures death by its length.

he believes one's memory survives
only if there's something to be
forgotten, which means there must
be something there ahead of it.

but slowly, one by one, the hoops
fall out and he realizes the tigers
will have to jump through him,
if he is to be set free forever.

thus the story ends: this is a work
of fiction and any resemblance
to actual persons, living or dead,
or events is entirely coincidental.

INSPIRATION

there is a poet swims with a turtle,
then, eating a cream turtle soup, wonders
whether he could write about its sense
of belonging, to the goalless ocean
or the beach and the hole where the eggs
are buried and born again forgotten.

the next day he decides to go and swim
with an octopus, the chameleon of the sea,
to see whether its colors could become his,
and that evening, eating raw octopus salad,
he believes he has absorbed enough to write
about its disdain for the unrhymed world.

yet all along he knows he does not have
the right thing, the ultimate answer to why
a poet gets inspired, until the third night
when he bites into a leather-like shark steak.

he wants to swim with sharks, to prove
they are not cold-blooded strategists but
like poets, when it comes to preying on words,
opportunists guided by ampullae of lorenzini.

that night his seat at the table is empty,
and while other hotel guests drink wine
and sway awkwardly in the rhythm of native
fire dances, the impervious sharks cruise
incuriously among turtles and octopuses.

DOWNSIZING

There were too many words
in your poem, the editor tells me
over the phone and I hate him instantly.

He knows he will not have to elaborate
because I shun from long conversations;
my mistake to call and ask him.

The only thing that comes to my mind is,
What do you mean "were;" there are,
I try painfully to entrap him.

Because you know which ones they are,
he says, and you'll take care of them.
Condense your suffering and surpass it.

Fine, I say, just to end the exchange.
Listen, he backtracks; I don't mean your stuff
isn't strong. It's powerful but disturbing.

*

What he wants me to do is have
a reader feel the pain without feeling
the need to understand it; otherwise,

one would be induced to stay with it
beyond the reading. But, like me, one
realizes it's hard to do so and still turn

the pages. He'd like me to get adjusted to
this (new) world, always glances at my watch
to see whether I'm stuck in the old time zone.

Of course, he does not know, nor would he care,
that my natural readers are all gone by now,
and those around think I no longer exist.

Things would be so much better, for him,
and for me, if I got out of the war
with my leg in my hands, or my eyes poached.

There would be some veritable point worth
listening about; I could offer my prosthesis as
a technological marvel that opens new vistas.

I could hope that the nerve-tickling sensation
still in my brain may lead to a restoration
of my vision in a not so distant future.

*

Right now, the only thing I can do is cut
myself down to six lines, though I presume
he'll find the word "here" too pointed.

Days are here like months, months
are like years, years
like death, instantaneously eternal,
or, conversely, eternally instantaneous.

What a waste of life to end like this.
What a waste of paper to talk about this.

I M A G I (N I) N G

There are other poets, he said,
coming out of other wars,
with equally powerful stories
and their interesting local flair.
We have understood your predicament
and consider the theme to be exhausted;
it's a dead thing now, if I may put
it this way. You are alive and well,
and with time you'll be normal again,
so turn to other things to write about
and let the past stay in the past.

not an entirely safe supposition,
I thought, for the other night I saw
myself on television, a fleeting camera
freeze as if something got stuck
or the man holding it did not know
what to do next, perhaps trying to guess
whether the next frame could be grislier
and cut out because deemed inappropriate,
or less catching and thus a waste of tape.

so, what was I doing on the evening news,
my face covered in plaster like a clown's,
a painted streak of blood appearing

out of my receding hair and branching
down my face, the same leaden stare
of a wounded animal at something not
there, as if I had been dropped again,
ten years later, into the instant scene
of another war in another land—

I thought of calling the station
to say that I was not part of that war,
that a mistake must have been made,
the reports got mixed somehow, or used
intentionally to create a desired effect,
but then I realized that I was
normal again and could easily write
about something I was not part of, just
another imaginary me remembering me—

PRETENSE

My friend, a poet and part time
lunatic like me, writes
he can't get pebbles out of his shoes
to roam Canada freely.

My first shoes after the war
were sandals mother made of a car tire
with sides looped up, punctured
and crisscrossed with braided rope.

I had to go to school
when the street mud was ankle deep,
but that quickly made me
a shining example of the people's state.

He calls me a few days later.
I'll be going back, he says.
Pebbles in your shoes are too much, I ask.
What pebbles? My mother's gone.

In my vision I run backwards
barefoot, my mother's words echo, her hair
pulled back by a soldier, the knife
glinting, You forgot your shoes.

Uprooted from myself now, I still pretend
that my never worn, perfectly polished
Johnston & Murphy boots in the closet
will be enough to stave off foreseen pictures.

HOPE

every day I find a piece
of my flesh in bed come morning;

I run, frenzied and naked, to the mirror
to see which part of me is missing.

I have been losing weight, but
there are no visible holes, no bleeding.

yet, each piece, usually the size
of a large stew cube, looks alive;

at times, I think, the muscle fiber
twitches, as if still fed blood by my heart.

every night I am in a long corridor,
the same woman on a stretcher next to me;

a surgeon stands between us and asks:
Does anyone know where her leg was

blown off; and she grabs his sleeve,
her fingers scorched: He stole it, doc . . .

I wrote a poem about this and had
my friend read it, hoping forlornly

he would take my falling apart
factually. two weeks later he calls

and pronounces: Postmodernism is dead.
What are you, a frustrated vegetarian?

but I am not, a vegetarian, I mean.
then again, maybe there's hope some

good comes out of all this, for when I
die I'll be just clean bones and a soul.

WAKE

the dead are already used
to being dead and gone,
so what am I doing
trying to keep them around

in this one-bedroom mind
of mine, their memory is
slowly drying out like ice
cubes in my tiny refrigerator

at night I turn the pages
of an album with photos of shoes,
shirts, sweaters, pants, belts,
as if shopping through a catalog

and I think I recognize something,
my jacket, for instance, a distinct ink
mark I see on the breast pocket, shrapnel
holes like cigarette burns dotting the sleeve

I sit with them, tell them stories,
those meant to purge us at the end,
then I eat and drink sumptuously,
mindless of food just going through me

THE WALL

one by one they would come
every night to buy back their acts
from me, as if they had the right
of passage through the scabbed wall
of the crypt, my colorless eyes
straining to arrest their successive faces,
my mind retrieving their footsteps

    —Marvin, who got so distraught looking
at those names, Albahari, Bloom, Klein,
Weinstein, thousands carved in the wall,
a fatefully neat alphabetical order,
that he kept drinking himself to oblivion
even when the plane carried him off
into thin air, then dropped on a beach
among sweaty faces and beer bellies
that with the swelling billows barked
the same unearthly words, Alle raus. Schnell.

    —Larry, who leaned against the wall,
his hands, long fishing poles,
thrust into bottomless pockets,
his eyes, two forsaken blue openings
in the stormy sky, trying to angle
for the words whose extraneous sounds
swam now toward another darkness

—Nekad sam mislio da čak i kroz to
mogao bih proći nježno ko zvijezda
okrećući se, okrećući
u dubokom miru njezina svjetla—
at the end shut, as if knowing the heavens,
unfathomed and done, snuffed out the light.

—Erica, her back and palms pressed
against the wall, as if to stop it
from crumbling down, while the lake's moon
shimmered in her eyes and the warm night
breeze played absently with her coppery perm,
waiting to regain her composure after a poet
from Greece, with a bulging golden helios
on his chest, declared he would rather make
love to her body/boy/guard/friend.

they would all come, one by one,
those still around, and those already gone,
Robert, Donald, Cynthia, Gregory, John—
I call them now; "I do not wish to remember
anything," I want to tell them, but
their ready-made line, "It's good to know
you're alive," keeps rewinding the memory,
and every night I stare at my face impressed
in the wall that just smiles at me crookedly

BARTER

A fellow poet has died
In a nursing home we used to call
Snow White, and I am still alive
Resisting the same fate.

The last time I saw him
We stood in line, having met
In one of the safe alleys, two dogs
Sniffing for any whiff of food.

He always believed that I was
Rational to the point of madness,
I, on the other hand, that he was mad
To the point of supreme rationality.

It didn't help us much that day,
Especially when he said,
Shuffling his feet but going nowhere,
Like a penguin with a dying battery,

"Who will sing," my dear friend,
"The song of those who are no more
But who passed this way
With a song on their lips?"

You are stealing from your own poems,
I remarked, speaking slowly
So the damp winter air
Would not make my teeth ache.

He had his front tooth missing,
From eating tin cans, he joked,
And his words whistled, the sound
Projectiles made jarring one's reflexes.

As we ran across the deserted intersection,
A small plastic bag with variegated beans
In his hand keeping the rhythm
Like a metronome, he lisped to me,

You wouldn't happen to have
Some toilet paper at home?
And I couldn't bring myself to tell
Him I no longer had a home.

I can give you a copy of my book,
I said. He looked at me, his skin,
Sickly yellowish, acquiring a sudden
Reddish tinge of one of the beans,

You are not suggesting, really . . . ,
He started. No, no, I assure you;
I'd like you to read it. First, at least.
In that case I'll be honored to have it.

He stretched his skinny hand, the bag
With beans swaying ceremonially in the air.
Please, take this. I have plenty,
And I can't eat this stuff anyway.

I took a battered copy out of my overcoat
And put the mercurial bag quickly
Into the same pocket. We shook hands,
Two people grinning after a good trade.

And now when I read in the paper
That no other books except his own
Were found in his dilapidated nursing home
Room, I smiled contentedly.

REASONING

I sat in the park
and watched a boy run
around the shimmering pond,
a huge plastic fighter jet
in his hand shone in the sun
with painful realness.
He held it with his thumb
and his index finger
as if it were a fragile bird,
yet let it dive fiercely
and climb up again,
the echo making me flinch
after each vocal bomb
he dropped, forcing two ducks
to scatter twice or thrice,
then grow indifferent
and go about their business,
the erratic swim in circles.

Sitting on a tree stump
on the other side of the pond,
his mother would wave
to him each time he went by,
then continue to stare
anxiously at the empty sky,

her eyes, I surmised, wishing
to lock in a real plane
before our scream was drowned
in its invisible wake.

Yet, was I wrong; was she,
in fact, waving to me
to tell me I was safe, just
casual part of her son's play?

When the boy was again
between his mother and me,
I leaned forward and yelled,
Who's the enemy?
He halted, his hand still up,
the jet hovering above,
arrested for a moment
like a pheasant shot by a hunter
sporting himself on Sunday.
You, he shouted. No one else is here.

THE SHAPE

the outlines on the Market Street
West were still visible,
the head an unevenly inflated balloon,
hands half-raised as if trying
to surrender or hold down the earth,
one leg bent slightly in the knee,
a wishful step never made
or a one-legged frog kick aborted,
the lines of the left foot fading,
not fully connected perhaps to allow
the breath some kind of fair passage

my shape was never chalked, the position
being utterly irrelevant, the angle
not even remotely predictable for those
who, if returning, had to run by again

so I lay down and filled the balloon,
inhaling the warm rancid blacktop,
my eyes staring at the crimson puddle
that broke out of the white boundary,
and I clenched my fists to fit the curve
that formed a swollen fingerless hand

I lay there motionless, waiting
for them to come at night and carry me
away, a figure on the cooling pavement
whose framed shape was a perfect match

GRATEFULNESS

(SEQUEL)

those who banished me think
I should be grateful to them
because I ended up on the island
that surely looks like heaven

those who took me in think
I should be grateful to them
because they believe they got me
out of something that was surely hell

(PREQUEL)

Conceived in April, when the Germans
attacked, I always thought, as a child,
I was the product of accident or fear
and shouldn't be grateful to anyone.

At home mother would say we should give
thanks to God for the bread we ate;
in school teachers claimed we must thank
the party for the fields rich with wheat.

(PREQUEL TWO)

Looking at the clothes, touching
them gently as if her fingers could
identify her husband's, she said,
I am so grateful you came with me.

Her dreamy eyes I loved once madly
did not see me beyond that moment,
and I was grateful she hadn't read
in mine a pained flash of crazed desire.

(SEQUEL TWO)

One day here I dropped some money
in a man's cup, whose stare soared
indifferently toward the leaden sky,
and he looked at me through me,

and whispered, I can see you are
the grateful one, which almost made
me snatch the cup and dig out half
of what I had generously put in.

(SEQUEL THREE)

You do not really die, my hostess
remarked, her perfume laying siege to me,

if you survive in someone's memory,
and that's something to be grateful for.

I was an exhibition piece in the room,
to be remembered briefly the next day
during a phone chat, but I went home
laughing to write a nice thank-you note.

FALLOUT

though life now seems to be repackaged
again neatly and the sign This End Up
points in the right direction, words
that haven't expired are the unedited pain

: we are sentenced to our own understanding
: we are condemned by our own versions,
    envious of each other's survival
    together still in our separate loneliness

—we sit at the table, two players
waiting for the other's time to run out,
and as I chase the last pod on my plate
I wonder which part of me will leave first

: my heart, sick of circulating my blood
: my mind, tired of negotiating with my heart,
    nothing to do with the moment you know
    you cheated death without knowing

—you do not want to remember anything,
and I remind you constantly of everything,
those nights on the ribbed cement floor
when I'd make a vague attempt to cover
my fear of shells with passion, peel

your eyes off the ceiling that trickled
semen dust and get out of the box
where every word was a muscle spasm

: you eat in silence abandoned in time
: I eat in silence cast away in space,
    I have the words but have lost the tenses,
    my heart skips a beat, a thought skipping me

—I stood in the cross wires, I want
to say, looking at a dot become a sun,
my vessel opened like petals and I
saw, wrapped in light, the inner landscape

UNANSWERED

why was I at the time
of war so obsessed with sex /

the eyes catching the motion
of someone crossing her legs
to penetrate the dark fissure
before the walls caved in again;
following the fingers that pulled
forlornly at the button of a blouse,
spying on the heaving mound;
the erections that would begin
in the thighs, their rippled quivering
like that of a horse trying
to shake off sweat driven flies /

Whenever feeling powerless,
Or cowed, or even victorious,
Men, she said, reading my look
while we were sitting in the cellar
one humid rainy afternoon
and she lifted the hem of her skirt
to wipe off the sweat on her forehead,
tiny globes I saw as passion beads,

Always yearn for this primitive,
Yet ultimate form of dominance /

I didn't know what caused
my hard-on, her gesture,
so innocent and yet so mindless,
or my desperate attempt to avoid
getting up and going as if on a walk
into the next cubicle to urinate
noisily into a huge tin bucket /

was that the right answer
telling me how senseless everything
was, or simply human nature
that parted company with reality /
?

SELFISHNESS

War, they've said so often, is cancer,
And now your cancer is war as well.

I lie next to you consumed by the desire
to restore the balance of life
and death, though knowing I have
no control over either, yet challenging
the memory of all the places
we used to die at, sweaty and breathless,
a cemetery, under the table
on a cold linoleum floor in your friend's kitchen,
or between the rocks while the salty breeze
pricked our skin with hordes of invisible ants.

would I have thought that something
I held cupped in my hand
like a ripened pear could be plucked off
leaving a line, a kind of unfinished thought,
the way your eyes were in the freezing cellar
when I wanted desperately to live again

your body whose shape I thought
I knew by heart, every curve and ridge,

every crevice, looks now like a plant
beaten constantly by winds on one side only.

I wonder whether it's your fear of me or my life
or my fear of you and your thought of dying
that makes me think I could have coped
more easily had that part of you
been taken away by a grenade.

IN / SIGHT

it's the hand with a comb suspended
in the air, its shadow on the wall
holding a straight razor poised
above its semblance target, tufts
of hair on his head, his marble gaze
fighting off the ceiling's descent,
his wheezing in concert with the draft
breathing curtain, that arrests me
as I walk by in the pasteurized light,
my parabolic memory trying once more
to have me curve death's axis.

my body reversed, a red disk inching
toward the heart in the mirror, I
jumped out of the frame, the coated glass
having turned into bladed shards.

which reflection do the optic nerves
recollect, the one taken or the one
translated, when to cross the pain's arc
one has to see the circumference of fate:
the lines had been drawn long before
the mind could outrun the blind spots
and make one think he was spared obliquely.

THE FILM

maybe all this is so
because he sleeps on the wrong side
of the rainbow

the electrical waves
crashing against the mind that mixes
dead colors

and the wires
twanging in the hollow chambers are
the echo driven spasm

the film burns
and the screen becomes a dilated pupil
eaten by a widening hole

the nerves
still spun on a clattery take-up spool
a snapped lizard's tail

the sound track
trapped in the shutter fades out in a drone
it's about time you wake up

yet he senses
if he opens his eyes he'll be caught
in the beam

unable to tell
whether his leg in the last frame was torn off
or just went to sleep again

WRITTEN

the unbound
  unpaginated death

                    words
                    now
                    need

/ in the mind's railed
space

                    to arrest
                    the palm's life
                    line

/ for the memory
unreadable
scars

                    that / what
                    in the passage
                    of time got
                    to / at you
                    if it started
                    as a simple motion
                    / let's say / of a hand
                    that felled a tree
                    ,and there

in the air / vacant
like the margins / no
-thing sustained / yet
more than enough
to undo the balance

your fate written
transversally

coming back
at / to
you

a fibrous pulp
once
,dried pressed
surface

only
/ reading the leaves
that whisper
about the geometry
of ascension

COUNTERPOINT

1.

you should know
        because you remember
or: you should not remember
        because you know

it is this because
        that causes that because
but: it is that because
        that cancels out this because

thus: maybe the time has come
        for you to forget
and the why of a journey will be
        the journey of a why

2.

yet, to know what one has found
        or did not want to find
to grasp the meaning of exile
        or exile the meaning itself

I have learned to subtract
     a forgiven life from an unforgiving death
and I have learned to add
     an unforgiving life to a forgiven death

even if I were to realize that
     someone had forced me to be lost,
that words would tell me
     what a door was but never where

3 .

would we still be able to escape
     a halved memory,
a story told that some day
     is going to be untold,

when words cannot be there
     to help us throw off
the pursuers of reversed fate and
     see when all has been done:

a passage to answers not to be
     found on chartered maps,
a passage to questions not asked
     by those who do not travel beyond themselves

ETERNITY

mother's bedtime stories always ended
with the same droning phrase:
And they lived happily ever after,
and when I asked her, my eyes half closed,
painting on our bare bedroom wall
a garden with shiny green lawns,
golden paths, sparkling fountains,
birch trees, and a bower where a maiden
lay on a bier hemmed by roses and lilies,
that means for ever ever,
the whole eternity,
she'd say: Yea, yea, but you have
To die first, for a while only,
Then someone comes on a white horse,
Gives you a kiss, you wake up,
And live forever; that's it, and now
It's your time to sleep.

she'd turn off the light,
and the sorcerous street lamp made
the tree's arms dash on the ceiling
just like father's did against her face,
her breathless cries in the kitchen
drowned by the blaring and puffing
of steam dragons at the steel mill.

I'd put the pillow over my head and run
into a garden trimmed in gold to sit
among rabbits, birds, butterflies, and fawn.

no one ever came to rescue her,
not even when she lay in a limy room,
with tubes and wires mixing her memory
of what battle she was going through,
her blood graying, eaten by debris,
while I held a receiver in another world,
and the thump of skysweepers I had fled
reverberated again in my metallic throat.
Remember, her morphine voice
trailing across the ocean floor,
How you wanted proof when you were little
Of living happily ever after,
The whole eternity? I was a poor story
Teller, always made you see what our fate
Was going to be. No tales left now
To hide in. No white horses. Only
These rime walls, around, and in me.
But maybe eternity won't be put on hold
If you come and give me a kiss good night

A REMINDER

this cold damp november night
trees are naked shapes waving
their arms behind barbed wire

the leaves, wet and bloodied,
I bring in stuck to my soles,
acidized tongues gone mute.

there's a mocking bird perched
in my head, its mimic calls
a beguiling relief of memory:

I would swim the ocean to save
you, I told her. a heroic phrase
to envelop cowardliness or helplessness.

Take the plane, son; it's faster,
her voice, imploded in my chest,
a reminder life was not a metaphor

for dying, the means of effacement
words that would mercifully forgive us
what we could not forgive ourselves.

my memory has become my sin,
fed maniacally by every breath,
itself a transient pardon of death.

A BALLAD

I have stood on the ground
turned inside out

I have smelled burned flesh
to drive away my monstrous hunger

I have walked among the dead
myself a breathing dead body

I have slept standing up
like an animal ready to run

I have dreamed I didn't wake up
unworried whether I was dead or not

I have tried to forget about myself
to make their scopes lose sight of me

I have failed to balance words
and the wounds still deeper than time

I have never managed to tell my mother
I was sorry for the pain I'd caused her

I have not been there when I thought
I was helping her to live her dying

I have missed my death at ten all two
and that's when my watch stopped moving

A SHORTCUT

I woke up one night to find
an angel sitting at the foot
of my bed and holding my coat.
I came to take you with me,
he said. You've suffered enough.
It's time you have some peace.

Was it necessary for you to come,
I asked. He smiled, or so I thought,
and said, Would you like someone else?
Snapping his invisible fingers, he
turned into a reddish burly man
I met in a bar once who claimed war
was a historical necessity to clear
the air. Truth, he exclaimed, is
at that point completely irrelevant.
He raised the glass, his little
and ring finger curiously hidden.

I can be your father, the angel
said and I heard the shoes click.
His torso swayed in the air, my coat,
over his shoulders now, resembling
the wings of a giant bat. The shoes
go click-a-click, the angel chanted,

and save the owner's life, your life,
my life, in the steamy Obersturm-a-
sturm-and-bon-a-bann-führer's office.

There suddenly was humming behind me,
and, turning, I saw camouflaged trees
advance toward me, the ghosts
dancing to the beat of his song.

Let us go, the angel said. We have
a train to catch, so we'll take
a shortcut. I looked at the mine
field ahead and then at him again.
Don't worry, my friend, he whispered
and winked, or so it seemed to me.
Nothing ever killed a man twice.

I took a deep breath and followed,
my airy legs almost waltzing.

EPI/LOGOS

there i was trading words for life
        hoping they'd live beyond themselves
i had seen the truth but never claimed
        to be the one to have touched it

death was sleeping in my bed
        pretending it kept it warm for me
while i lay frozen on the table
        with a piece of lead in my forehead

there were flat shapes there words
        could not negotiate fault lines
i thought would some day close and heal
        as if the senses had never fractured

was that the point where i was let go
        to stumble spectrally through a tunnel
into the exploding frameless light
        unaware darkness also left me blind

whatever the visionless roads that brought
        me to this stage that is my fate
words imprinted on the skin now
        lesions on the membrane of memory

and if this is what i have to be to know
        what i was not to be the only thing
left to tell Shakespeare is *i have lost*
        my mind trying to save my head

ACKNOWLEDGMENTS

The following poems have appeared in print and electronic journals, sometimes in a slightly different form: "The All," "Balance," "Barter," "Beyond," "Collateral," "Conversion," "Death," "Deliverance," "Dyeing," "The Egg," "Epi/Logos," "Eternity," "FALLout," "Fear," "The Film," "Imagi(ni)ng," "Inheritance," "A Leap," "Life," "Metaphorplication," "The Pit," "Pretense," "Reasoning," "Selfishness," "The Shape," "A Shortcut," "The Smell," "Suitcases," "Unanswered," "Wake," "The Wall," and "Written." Grateful acknowledgment is made to the editors of the following journals: *Borderlands: Texas Poetry Review*, *Chase Park*, *Colere*, *Concrete Wolf*, *Dream Catcher* (UK), *Futures*, *Glass Tesseract*, *Inkwell*, *Luna*, *magma poetry* (UK), *The Mid-America Poetry Review*, *The Mochila Review*, *Nassau Review*, *The Paumanok Review*, *Phantasmagoria*, *Poetic Voices*, *Poetry International Web* (the Netherlands), *Poetry Motel*, *The Progressive*, *The Raven Chronicles*, *Red Wheelbarrow*, *Reflections*, *Sonora Review*, *Wavelength*, and *Wind*. I'd like to express my gratitude to Jonathan D. Rabinowitz, whose understanding and patience went far beyond the call of duty. Also, thanks to Bruce Urquhart, Robert Karmon, Susan Marshall, Barbara Simon, Richard J. Newman, Barry Fruchter, Michael Steinman, and Ruzha Cleaveland for their reading and support.